I'm Not Invited

Other Books by Claire Burbank

WWW.CLAIREBURBANK.COM

Other Titles by Claire Burbank
Bullying (The Bully Book)
Claire Burbank Book Collection V1
Claire Burbank Book Collection V2
Five Crows
Sassy Tomatoes
Mo Lemont
Loop of Dreams
Magically Acquainted

I'm Not Invited

CLAIRE BURBANK

Burbank Ventures
LLC
Nottingham, NH

Copyright © 2018 by Claire Burbank. All rights reserved. This book or any portion thereof may not be reproduced or used in any manner whatsoever without the express written permission of the publisher except for the use of brief quotations in a book review.

Amelia Maskin, Aqua Blaire Juniper, Beanie Moss, Claire Burbank, Grapes the Monkey, Isaac's Diary, Mister Bobby Superhero, Mo Lemont, Rosie MacDonald, Sassy Tomatoes are trademarks of Claire Burbank.

Contents

Other Books by Claire Burbank — vii
Acknowledgements — ix

1. A NEW START — 1
2. SECRETS — 7
3. INTERROGATION — 13
4. DRAMA — 19
5. UNFRIENDED — 25
6. TRUE FRIENDS — 31
7. THE FRIEND SEEKERS — 37

Acknowledgements

To: My family for supporting everything I do and to everyone who read one of my books and learned lessons about **bullying**, **friendship** and **treating each other as we would want to be treated.**

1

A NEW START

Ellie, Reyna and I have been best friends since we met in kindergarten for our first year of Mountain View Elementary. I'm Amelia Maskin and I live in Fairmount New Jersey. I'm eleven years old and I'm going into the sixth grade with my two best friends! I'm so excited to be big kids with my BFFs! We are going to have so much fun! ...or at least that's what I thought...

I heard from some other people that

there were going to be a lot of new kids joining sixth grade, which I was kind of feeling neutral about. I was ready to go to school knowing everyone, like the way it was since we were younger, but at the same time I was ready to make some new friends!

"Amelia!" Reyna exclaimed as I walked onto the bus.

"Hi!" I replied, ready for the first day of school.

Reyna and I always ride the bus together since our houses are near each other, and we meet Ellie at school.

"I'm kind of nervous since the seventh graders said there was a lot of homework," I told Reyna.

"Well at least you're in a class with Ellie!" she retorted, feeling jealous. "I'm all on my own!"

"That's okay, you have a really nice teacher," I assured her.

When we got to school, we met up with Ellie excitedly and then headed off to our classes.

I didn't recognize two people as I walked

into class. One was a girl, which I was kind of excited about since I might be able to be friends with her!

My teacher seemed to be really nice, and some of my classmates made good impressions while others made the poor choice of looking "good" in front of their fellow classmates by behaving badly (but really, they were the ones who looked bad).

The only time to really socialize was lunch and recess, and these two times were pretty much the same as last year besides the fact that kids were finding tables to sit at during lunch.

The table that Ellie, Reyna, our other friends and I sat at was a specific table, which was the table in the middle of the cafeteria. I think of us as nice, well-behaved and welcoming girls since all of us were open to letting new girls sit at our table and hang out with us at recess. We even talked to each other about how we should invite people to our table that day. Though, no girls at our school are very exclusive, we all let anyone sit at our tables if they want to and include them in our conversations.

When I saw the girl that was new in my class, I called her over and told her to sit next to Ellie and me. She was actually very kind and funny, and she told us about her old school. I knew that we would be very good friends.

She told us her name was Baylee, and we could tell she was very sassy, which was a characteristic that made her unique and funny. Though Baylee was friends with all of us, she hung out with me most of the time. I was glad to have a new friend that was friends with Ellie and Reyna, too.

During homeroom, Baylee and I were always partners when it came to assignments and worksheets. Sometimes I showed her my strange side with my weird voices and phrases, and she was kind of weirded out by it. But, you know, not everyone is amused by my uniqueness like Ellie and Reyna. They appreciate it and think it's awesome. Those are true friends right there.

The first few weeks of sixth grade were very different from fifth grade, with lockers, switching classes and all. Baylee had become one of my best friends that I hung out with all the time. Sometimes she seemed annoyed at me, but everyone gets grumpy...right?

2

SECRETS

The first half of the year went by very quickly because of having three teachers and switching classes a lot. At lunch and recess, during the middle of the year, Baylee started telling secrets to Ellie and Reyna.

"What are you guys talking about?" I asked Baylee one time.

"Oh, nothing," she replied.

Another time during lunch, the three of them were nodding and clapping after whispering to each other. They tried to make it look like they weren't hiding anything, but I knew they were talking behind my back.

"Are you talking about me?" I asked them, feeling left out. "It's not fair that I'm not part of the conversation."

"No, we're just talking about the dance coming up at the end of the year," Baylee explained. "We just don't want the teachers to hear."

"Can I hear what you're talking about, too?" I questioned.

"Sure!" Ellie replied.

They started talking about the dance, but I knew that it wasn't what they were talking about before.

Also, during recess, Baylee was talking to Ellie and Reyna separately to tell them something.

"Can I talk to you about something?" she asked Ellie when her, Reyna and I were hanging out.

They went and talked on the swings without Reyna and me.

I'm Not Invited

I sighed.

"I'm sure they aren't talking about us," Reyna told me.

"Yeah," I retorted. "Me too,"

I knew they were excluding me from something, I just didn't know what. I also didn't know why. I knew they would just make up excuses or something like that, so I left it alone.

When I came home that day, I lay on my bed with my dog Nugget.

My family and I first got Nugget when I was four years old. He was just a puppy and we loved him since the day we laid our eyes on him. We named him Nugget because he was very small and the color of a chicken nugget. Every time someone asks "Did you name him Nugget because he loves chicken nuggets?" We answer, "No, he actually hates chicken nuggets! We named him that because of the color of his fur."

Nugget is my support animal when I'm feeling sad.

"Why are they hiding something from me behind my back?" I asked Nugget, petting his soft fur. "I didn't do anything wrong, so why can't I know what they're talking about?"

My parents always told me I was tough, but the tears that I had been holding in from that day of secrets streamed down my face. I had never felt so sad and betrayed because of the drama at school before.

My mom heard me crying and came into my room.

"Why are you crying?" she asked in a sympathetic voice. "You never get upset."

She came and sat on my bed with me as I pet Nugget.

"Reyna, Ellie, and Baylee are keeping secrets from me," I told her.

"Really?" she asked. "But they're your best friends!"

"I know, right?" I answered, tears still rolling down my face.

"Why don't you ask them what they're talking about?" she suggested.

I sniffed. "I've tried, but they keep making excuses."

I hugged Nugget, feeling like I had no real

friends anymore. Why would they leave me out?

"Aw, give me a hug," Mom said, leaning in for an *I feel sorry for you* hug. "It's a good thing you have Nugget."

I chuckled. "Yeah, he's my REAL best friend."

"I'll text Reyna's mom and ask her what's going on," she told me.

"Okay," I agreed.

She went to the kitchen to grab her phone which was charging.

When she came back, she had a confused look on her face. "She said that there was no secret, and that Reyna will tell Ellie and Baylee that they'll include you in their conversations tomorrow."

"See, Reyna just doesn't want to make me feel bad," I answered angrily. "But hiding it from me is just making me feel worse!"

"Well, at school tomorrow, just say that you want to know what they're hiding and that it won't make you feel bad," Mom suggested.

"Okay," I agreed, "but I *do* feel bad."

"You know what, let's go out for dinner," she replied. "And then for ice cream!"

"Really?" I asked her. "Thanks, Mom!"

"Anything for my favorite daughter," she answered.

"Mom, I'm your only daughter," I reminded her.

"I know," she said.

3

INTERROGATION

The next day, I decided that I would interrogate Baylee, Ellie, and Reyna one by one until someone spilled the beans. I knew that Ellie wasn't that great at keeping secrets, so I was sure she would crack at one point.

When I got on the bus that morning, I remembered that I could question Reyna on our way to school! So I went and sat with her, and when I first saw her face it looked very nervous. I guess she knew what was coming.

"I guess you know what I'm gonna ask you," I stated.

"Yup," she replied. "But it's not my fault, Baylee started it."

"So what's the secret?" I asked. "I won't be upset if you tell me."

"Baylee will be upset, though," she told me. "She told Ellie and me that we can't tell you, but I promise it's not about you."

"You guys aren't even trying to hide it," I retorted, tearing up. "We've been friends forever and you guys are telling secrets right in front of me! It's not fair!"

"I'm sorry, we never meant to hurt your feelings," Reyna sympathetically remarked. "We were trying to do the opposite because what we're *talking about* may hurt your feelings."

"Well, you're not hiding it very well," I told her, "and I didn't do anything wrong."

I turned away from her for the rest of the ride, upset that I didn't discover the secret my three best friends were hiding from me.

I could tell she felt bad, but I knew that Baylee wouldn't feel bad based on her sassy personality. I was really disappointed in my friends. I trusted them and expected more from them, and they turned on me. Yes, I felt sorry for myself, but it was for a reason.

I decided that my next target for interrogation was Ellie because I felt more confident in getting the secret out of her than Baylee.

When I entered my homeroom, Baylee and Ellie were talking to each other AGAIN. So I went up to Ellie and asked, "Can I talk to you for a second?"

"Sure!" the peppy Ellie replied.

"What were you, Reyna, and Baylee secretly talking about yesterday?" I asked. "No one will tell me."

"It really wasn't important," she explained. "I'm sorry we didn't include you."

Did someone give her lying lessons?

"If it wasn't important, than why don't you tell me?" I retorted, getting kind of angry.

"I can't," she argued. "Baylee won't—"

"—let you tell me," I interrupted. "I know. Reyna told me that."

"I'm sorry," she apologized. "We didn't mean to turn this into middle school drama."

"I know," I replied. "I'm just…disappointed."

And then I walked away. That's right, I played the disappointed card. I decided I wanted to take a little break from interrogation, so I would question Baylee at recess.

During lunch, the three of them didn't tell secrets…at least in front of me. I could tell that they were still untrustworthy when I came back from the bathroom and they were whispering. While I WAS in the cafeteria, though, it was very awkward because they all knew I was upset with them.

When it was finally recess, I pulled Baylee aside to question her.

"So…what's the secret?" I asked. "I asked Ellie and Reyna and they both said that you started it."

"Well, I'm sorry, but we don't have to include you in everything," she replied. "We didn't mean to make you feel bad, we didn't even want you to know about it."

Excuse me? Did she just say that she didn't *have* to include me? I thought we were best friends!

"Can you just tell me what it is?" I begged. "I didn't do anything, and I deserve to know."

"Okay, fine!" she finally agreed. "The secret is…"

4

DRAMA

"—I'm throwing a birthday party and I could only invite two people," she confessed. "So I decided to invite Ellie and Reyna."

"Okay," I said softly. "That's all I wanted to know, th—thank you."

I walked away, holding in my tears. I was kind of expecting that answer, but I was hoping my prediction wasn't accurate. I mean, couldn't she have talked her mom into inviting ONE MORE PERSON? I felt very betrayed after that, even more than before. I mean, how could my two best friends let this happen and whisper about it right in front of me? I mean, not *everything* is Baylee's fault.

During recess, I held in my tears by playing with one of my other friends, Sarah. She's super funny, so I was hoping that she could help me hold in my sadness before it came out and made my eyes red. Luckily, it worked, and I kept my mind off the drama by completely focusing on my schoolwork for the rest of the day.

When I came home, I immediately went to my room to get help from Nugget the support dog. That was when I let the tears flow and the questions in my head be thought about.

How was Baylee ever my friend?

Why would she do this to me?

Why are they treating me like I'm not their friend, too?

Is there another reason that I'm not invited?

If so, what is that reason?

I pet Nugget as I thought through these

I'm Not Invited

questions, wondering what the unknown answers were.

"Friend troubles?" my mom asked as she opened the door to my room.

"Yep," I answered.

She came and sat on the side of my bed again. "What happened?"

"It turns out Baylee is throwing a birthday party and she isn't inviting me," I explained. "And she's inviting Ellie and Reyna."

"Aww, honey," she said. "You know what, for your birthday party, you should invite Ellie and Reyna and not Baylee."

"How is that solving anything?" I asked, chuckling a little bit. "Revenge isn't the answer."

"I know, I'm sorry," she laughed. "I'm not very good at this middle school drama stuff."

"It's okay," I replied. "Maybe I should hang out with other people for now, or try to hang out with them again and see Baylee's reaction. To see if she still wants to be my friend."

"You should be giving ME advice!" Mom exclaimed.

Nugget barked, seeming to agree.

We laughed. I was feeling better already, like I could handle this problem.

I decided I wouldn't make up a plan this time, I would just see how things went. I still had no idea why Baylee didn't invite me. Maybe because she didn't like me, but why? I had so many questions, and I didn't know when they would be answered.

When I came on the bus the next morning, I didn't know what to expect. Would it be awkward? I didn't know.

"Amelia!" Reyna exclaimed, patting the space next to her.

I sat down next to her, glad that she still wanted to sit with me.

"You know, just because Baylee isn't inviting you to her birthday party doesn't mean you, Ellie, and I have to stop being best friends," she assured me. "We can't let this new girl get in between our friendship."

"I agree," I answered. "I'm glad I have

good friends like you and Ellie that stay by my side."

She smiled. For the rest of the bus ride, we both listened to my music with my headphones connecter. We listened with our earbuds that we bought together at the mall one time. I was feeling way better, but at times I still had a sick feeling in my stomach when thinking about how much fun my friends were gonna have without me.

When I came into my classroom, as always, Ellie and Baylee were talking to each other. This time, I decided to try to talk with them. I mean we were still friends, even if Baylee didn't invite me to one thing. Maybe the excuse about only being able to invite two people was true. But that's still negative for me since she chose them over me.

"Hey guys," I greeted them.

"Hi!" Ellie replied.

"I have to go to the bathroom," Baylee told Ellie, totally ignoring me.

"What was that about?" I asked Ellie. "What did I do?"

"I have no idea, Reyna and I have no idea

why she's treating you like this," she explained. "Remember, I'm still one of your best friends. Right?"

"Of course," I agreed. "I just thought the four of us could be best friends."

"That can still happen!" Ellie told me. "Let me talk to her."

I like her positivity…but could it?

5

UNFRIENDED

That day was going by pretty smoothly, especially since Ellie and Reyna both assured me that we were all still best friends. Baylee, though...she made me question our friendship.

When lunch started, I saw Ellie, Reyna, and Baylee sitting at our usual table. I went and sat across from them as they were chatting away.

"Hi!" Ellie and Reyna exclaimed in unison. "Jinx!"

I laughed at their uniformity, and then I looked at Baylee. Her eyes were looking away from us while her expression was bored.

"I'm gonna go sit with Sierra," she said as she stood up from her seat.

I sighed. What did *I* do wrong that Ellie and Reyna didn't? She was kind of acting like a jerk by ignoring me like this and not inviting me to her birthday party while she was inviting my two other best friends. It was then that I decided that Baylee didn't deserve my friendship. She was treating me unfairly and I didn't want to be her friend anymore.

For the rest of lunch, Ellie, Reyna, and I ignored Baylee and talked like we did before Baylee came along.

Once recess started, I went right to the swings. Right when I sat down next to my fifth-grade friend Bella, I was interrupted by someone.

"Hey, can I talk to you for a second?" Baylee asked me.

"Yeah, sure," I answered.

Is this it? I thought. *Is she finally apologizing to me?*

"I don't know how to say this," she started, "but...can we not be friends anymore?"

"Why?" I asked, a little offended. "What did I do?"

"No, nothing, nothing at all!" she exclaimed. "It's just...some people don't mix."

"Okay," I replied. "Bye."

After that, I walked away. I guess you could say my wish came true...but not exactly the way I wanted it to. I mean, she said it in a nice way, but that still doesn't make it kind. You can't just say that you don't want to be friends with someone and think it's perfectly fine. I wouldn't have had a big problem with it if she hadn't invited my two best friends to her birthday party and still be friends with them and not me. It just wasn't fair.

That night, I texted Ellie and Reyna in our group chat that was titled *Besties*.

Besties

Amelia: So Baylee told me that she didn't want 2 B friends w/ me anymore @ recess

Reyna: She told us she was going to, right B4 she did & we said she shouldn't but she did anyway

Ellie: Yeah

Amelia: Y tho?

Reyna: Idk

Ellie: Yeah we do know she told us no more secrets

Reyna: Sry I didn't want to make her feel worse than she already does

Amelia: Thx but I do wanna know

Reyna: Ok

Ellie: She thinks ur annoying

Amelia: Oh

Reyna: I'm sorry she thinks that

Amelia: It's fine not everyone has 2 like me and as she said "some people don't mix"

Ellie: But it's not fine, that's not OK

Amelia: I'll be alrite

Reyna: Can I tell her the other thing?

Ellie: I think we have 2

Amelia: What?

Reyna: She said we have 2 choose u or her

Wait, what? She said that? She can't do that to three best friends that have been besties since kindergarten! Especially when she's brand new to Mountain View! This girl was really getting on my nerves! But I knew my friends would choose me...right? That's when I realized...that they never said that they weren't going to her birthday party, and also they were hanging out with her a lot even though she unfriended me! This could mean...that they would choose her over me!

6

TRUE FRIENDS

The next day was a Friday, which was usually my favorite day of the week.

This Friday though, was NOT my favorite day of the week. I was worried, mad, and upset at the same time. I was worried because there was the chance of Baylee stealing my two best friends, mad because of the same reason, and upset because we let the new girl get in between our friendship.

The beginning of the day was pretty

normal, I got my work done, I focused in class, I ate lunch. Then there was recess. Somehow all of the drama occurred at recess.

I was just swinging on the swings next to Bella when I noticed Ellie, Reyna, and Baylee talking.

"Oh, no," I thought, butterflies swarming in my stomach. "I bet they're talking about the friend-choosing incident."

While I was watching them, the conversation went from talking to arguing.

What are they talking about? I thought, confused.

When their conversation was over, I saw Baylee walk in a different direction from Ellie and Reyna, and Ellie and Reyna walking towards me.

"What happened?" I asked them when they reached me.

"Here, let me explain," Ellie insisted.

So here's what she told me the conversation was:

"So, who did you choose?" Baylee asked.

"Do we really HAVE to choose?" Reyna questioned.

"Yeah, why are you making us do this?" Ellie added.

"So I don't have to hang out with *Amelia*," Baylee answered, saying my name in an annoyed voice.

"What will happen if we choose Amelia?" Ellie asked.

"You're uninvited to my party and we won't be friends anymore," Baylee explained.

"Maybe we can hang out with you at school and Amelia out of school," Reyna suggested.

"No, Reyna, Amelia has been our best friend since forever," Ellie argued.

"So, what's your decision?" Baylee asked.

"We choose Amelia," Ellie and Reyna told her after a short discussion between the two of them.

"Fine," Baylee snapped. "See you never."

And then that was the end of their conversation.

"For one, thank you for choosing me," I

said, "and second of all, how could she? She acted like she had all control."

"I know," Ellie agreed. "I don't know how we were ever friends with her."

"Well, the important thing is that everything is back to normal," Reyna proclaimed, stopping us from becoming gossip girls.

"Yeah, that's true," I agreed. "I'm really glad the drama is over."

"Wait a second," Ellie said. "Look at Baylee."

We all looked over at Baylee, who was crying while sitting against the fence in the corner of the playground.

"Why is *she* crying?" I asked, not trying to be snobby, but just curiously.

"Probably because she lost her only guests to her birthday party," Amelia suggested. "Now I feel kind of bad for her."

"Same," Ellie and I agreed.

"She also doesn't have any friends anymore," I pointed out, raising all of our pity for her.

"I mean, she made a mistake," Ellie told us. "We have to help her out."

"But how?" I asked. "She just unfriended all three of us."

Amelia gasped. "I have an idea that I think might work!"
And then she explained to us her genius idea.

"Maybe we could find her a new friend that we think would hang out with her by questioning people and seeing what their personality is like," she explained. "When we find someone, they could hang out with her without us introducing her so Baylee doesn't know we did it. Since she wouldn't know it was us, she would think that she made a friend or two on her own. That would boost her confidence. What do you think?"

"I think that's a great idea!" I exclaimed. "We need a group name, like the Ghost Busters do."

"The Friend Busters?" Ellie suggested. "No, never mind."

"Ooh! I got it!" I exclaimed. "How about...the Friend Seekers!"

"Yeah!" my best friends agreed.

So that was it. The Friend Seekers were on our first mission to find Baylee some new friends.

7

THE FRIEND SEEKERS

Luckily, Ellie, Reyna, and I still had plenty of time that recess to find Baylee at least one new friend.

"We should go ask that girl over there if she would hang out with her," Ellie suggested, pointing to a girl that was sitting on a bench on her own.

"Yeah! We could cure both of their loneliness!" Reyna exclaimed.

We walked over to the girl and noticed she was upset, too.

"What's wrong?" I asked her sympathetically.

"I have no friends," she replied. "No one wants to hang out with me."

Ellie, Reyna, and I looked at each other, smirking.

"Well, there *is* another girl over there that has the same problem," Ellie explained. "She's upset, too."

"Maybe you could go over and try to be friends with her," Reyna suggested.

"She has no friends either?" the girl asked.

"Nope," I answered.

The girl wiped her tears away and took a deep breath. "Okay, I'll go over to her. Maybe then I'll finally have a friend."

"You go girl!" Ellie exclaimed.

Once she left to go meet with Baylee, I said, "Well that was easy."

"Yeah, she had the same exact problem!" Reyna agreed.

"Do you guys want to go try to find her another friend?" Ellie questioned. "It might not be as easy, but I think we can do it."

"Because we are..." I started, and then Ellie and Reyna joined in. "The Friend Seekers!"

We all stuck our fists in the air like superheroes, and then laughed at our unity.

We looked around at different groups of people, and couldn't find another person that was alone. So we started searching for people in groups of two.

"Ooh!" Reyna exclaimed. "There are two girls on the swings over there!"

We ran over to them and said hi.

"Hi!" they greeted back.

"So we were wondering if you guys could hang out with those two girls over there," I explained, pointing at Baylee and the other girl that was alone before.

"Sure, but why can't you guys hang out with her?" one of the girls on the swings asked.

"It's a long story," Ellie replied.

"Okay, we understand," the other girl kindly retorted. "We'll go hang out with them.

"Thank you so much, we appreciate it,"

Reyna thanked them. "They've both been struggling to find friends."

"No problem, we were kind of bored anyway," one of the girls told us.

So the girls kindly went to hang out with Baylee and the girl that was previously on the bench.

"I think our work here is done," I told my friends.

"I agree," Ellie proudly said.

"Look at them," Reyna told Ellie and I, pointing at Baylee and the three other girls we found.

They were all talking to each other, getting along like they had known each other for a while. I was happy that everything turned out well in the end. From that whole experience, I learned some things. I learned that Ellie and Reyna are true friends, that more people share the same problems in my school than I thought, and that some people just don't mix. What I would suggest to anyone that also isn't invited to something is that you didn't do anything wrong, and it will turn out okay in the end. Also, sometimes you might not have the right friends. Don't go with the friends or groups that you don't think are very nice just because they are cool or popular, go with the friends that you think are loyal and kind to you. That's the advice from me. The next time I'm not invited, I won't let it turn into middle school or high school drama. Just remember, nobody likes to be left out. I won't forget that the next time I'm not invited.

www.ingramcontent.com/pod-product-compliance
Lightning Source LLC
Chambersburg PA
CBHW070037040426
42333CB00040B/1700